The Greatest Love

Eva Peck

© 2016 by Rev. Eva Peck
All rights reserved
Except for any fair dealing permitted under the Copyright Act, no part of this book may be reproduced by any means without prior permission of the author and publisher.

Text and preparation for publishing: Eva Peck

Cover design: Eva Peck
Cover photography:
arztsamui at FreeDigitalPhotos.net and
Stuart Miles at FreeDigitalPhotos.net

Other photography:
Page viii: arztsamui at FreeDigitalPhotos.net
Author photo: Jindrich Degen, edited by Alex Peck

National Library of Australia Cataloguing Entry
Creator: Peck, Eva, author.
Title: The greatest love / Eva Peck.
ISBN: 9780992454999 (paperback)
Notes: Includes bibliographical references.
Subjects: God—Love.
 God (Christianity)—Love.
 Love—Religious aspects--Christianity.

For more information
and other available literature, visit
http://universal-spirituality.net/ and
http://www.pathway-publishing.org/

Dedicated to all those
who are hungering in their souls
for God's Love and Truth

Other Books in this Series

- The Problem of Sin and Evil
- The Bible as a Guide to Life
- Jesus the Christ – a New Look at His Identity and Mission
- Salvation
- Answers to Prayer
- Life After Death
- Fulfilment of Old Testament Types

For other related reading,
including free PDF downloads, visit
http://universal-spirituality.net/ and
http://www.pathway-publishing.org/

Contents

Introduction 1

God is Love 3

Human Beginnings 5

Natural Human State 8

Human Potential for Divinity 13

Human Love versus Divine Love 17

Prayer for Divine Love 22

Further Reading 25

Acknowledgements 27

About the Author 28

About Pathway Publishing 31

Introduction

The Greatest Love discusses various aspects of love that humans express towards each other, and the yet greater and far superior Love of God or Divine Love. It shows that humans were created basically good and have inherent in their hearts and souls a measure of love which if mutually practised and lived by would make our world a much happier place.

However, people can not only choose to live by precepts such as the Ten Commandments in the Judeo-Christian tradition or the Eightfold Path taught by the Buddha, which can be summed up by the Golden Rule of treating others as we ourselves wish to be treated, and the great commandment of loving one's neighbour as oneself. Humans also have the opportunity to pray for and receive God's Divine Love, which if cultivated in their souls and applied in their day-to-day actions enables them to love unconditionally as Jesus loved – including loving their enemies. It also transforms individuals at the soul level from humans

Introduction

created in God's image to new, divine creatures whose souls consist of divine substance.

Divine Love is indeed the greatest love – God's own Love, with which He so loved the world that He sent Jesus to make known to humanity the way to His Kingdom and immortality. And this way is through the very same Divine Love that God has made available to all His human children for the asking so that they can become at one with Him.

Readers are encouraged to consider the information presented here with open minds and hearts, and decide for themselves whether or not it resonates with them.

God is Love

God is Soul, composed of His greatest attribute, Divine Love, which is His very nature and essence. His other attributes include mercy, goodness, power, omniscience, and will (1 John 4:8, 16; Psalm 116:12; Deut. 4:31; Eph. 2:4-5). God as Soul is far more than the sum of His attributes.

God's attributes radiate from His great soul and flood the universe. So, when people say they live and have their being in God (Acts 17:28), they are technically in error, but they do live and have their being in the divine attributes that emanate from God and that He has placed in human souls.

God has a place in the Celestial Heavens, but His attributes are present everywhere and fill the universe, or even multiple universes that scientists postulate might exist. The earth is a tiny, indeed infinitesimal, portion of all that exists. Even the "heavens" or spirit world where humans go when they die is a subset of the entirety of Creation (Psalm 47:8; 53:2; 139:7-13).

God is Love

All humans are God's dear children regardless of their conduct or whether or not they are converted. God's Love and care extends to each and every one because they are His creatures and He has a wonderful plan for them, as we shall see.

The fact that humans are sinners and that some have wandered away from Him and became strangers makes them no less His beloved children, whom He is anxious to redeem (Matt. 5:45; Luke 6:35; 11:13). The Father's mercy is for all, and if some of His children do not choose to accept it, He respects their free will at all times, but His Love for them never ceases.

Human Beginnings

What makes humanity unique is a *soul or spirit essence* made in divine image. Human-like beings had existed on earth for eons of time, passing, like everything, through a long period of development. At some point they were given a human soul and consciousness. This led them to the realization of being a unique divine creation – in fact the highest and most wonderful of all earthly creatures and the objects of God's Love and tenderest care.

At the beginning of human history, our ancestors' soul had the potential of being transformed into divine substance. In other words, the first parents had the opportunity to receive divine nature and reach a state oneness with God and therefore immortality. This would have been accomplished by asking for and receiving Divine Love imparted by the Holy Spirit. In the book of Genesis, this is symbolized by the availability of the Tree of Life (Gen. 2:8-9). The resulting heart / soul transformation was later referred to by Old Testament prophets as a *new heart* or a *new spirit* (Jer. 24:7; Ezek. 11:19; 18:31; 36:26).

However, instead of gratefully accepting their Creator's offer, the first parents rebelled against their Maker and as a result lost this priceless opportunity (Gen. 3:22). After the initial disobedience, referred to in Christianity as "the Fall", humanity gradually descended into further sin and depravity (Gen. 6:5). Through it all, however, they never lost knowledge of the basic laws of morality and the small voice of conscience giving them an awareness of sin and wrongdoing.

Despite the Fall, God in His Love and mercy has provided two ways for the redemption of humanity and for all to ultimately reach a sinless and happy state of existence without suffering.

The first way is for the soul to be purified either in this life or after death in the spirit world, through obedience to commandments, self-discipline, and overcoming sin, until it reaches the state of perfection possessed by the first parents before their Fall. This is the way taught by prophets and teachers such as Moses, Mohammed and the Buddha.

The second way is through soul transformation by the Divine Love in response to earnest prayer. This Love of God not merely purifies the soul, but also transforms it into the essence of the Creator. As a result, the soul becomes aware of, and in possession of, immortality. This is the salvation that Jesus taught when he came to earth and became the Messiah.

Natural Human State

Humans have a dual nature – material (animal) and spiritual. Thus we have passions and feelings belonging to both realms. The soul, made in God's image, is what makes us into the greatest of God's creations. The material (animal) inclinations only become sinful if they violate the laws of God (1 John 3:4). When that happens, spiritual aspirations become dormant and the soul becomes encrusted with evil.

Since humans have a free will, each person can choose which of the two natures will predominate in their life. They can align with the spiritual mind and divine image in their souls and thus strengthen their spiritual nature; or they can indulge in sinful thoughts and actions, through which the soul becomes contaminated.

Since the Fall, or rebellion against God, humanity has largely followed the animal nature resulting in what the Bible calls the "works of the flesh," "desires of the sinful nature," or lusts and wrong motives leading to wars and animosities (Rom. 8:5-8;

Natural Human State

Gal. 5:16-21; James 3:14-16; 4:1-3) – its present natural state.

Being made in God's image, humans also possess certain attributes of God, including creativity and love. Natural love (as distinguished from God's Divine Love discussed in more detail later) is undoubtedly the greatest gift that God the Father has bestowed on humankind apart from the potential of receiving the Divine Love. Without natural love in human hearts, the world would be in a very unhappy state. Love brings people into unity and a greater state of happiness than any other human quality. The different types of natural love include:

- Love for God: Both Moses and Jesus exhorted people to love God with all their heart, soul, mind and strength (Deut. 6:5; Luke 10:27).
- Parental love: Mother's love is one of the strongest loves, yet it too can fail – in contrast to God's Love which will never fail (Isa. 49:15).

- Self-love in the proper sense: If we are to love our neighbor as ourselves (Luke 10:27), proper sense of self-worth is necessary. This is not the same as selfishness or self-indulgence.
- Married love: This includes mutual respect and mutual submission (Eph. 5:21).
- Sibling love and love for relatives: The Old Testament portrays this in the touching story of Joseph, whose love for his brothers shines through despite their hate and betrayal (Gen. 42-45); and the mutual love and friendship between two widows – Ruth, the Moabite, and her Israelite mother-in-law, Naomi (Book of Ruth).
- Love of children for their parents: The expression of this love includes obedience and honor when under parental authority, and respect and honor throughout life. A blessing is promised for honoring one's own parents (Ex. 20:12; Prov. 6:20; Eph. 6:1-3; Col. 3:20).

- Friendship love: An inspiring Old Testament example is David's friendship with Jonathan (1 Sam. 20).
- Love for neighbor: The second great commandment – to love one's neighbor as oneself – includes in its broadest sense every human being (Lev. 19:18; Luke 10:27-37).
- And even love for enemies: This is the most challenging, but Jesus exhorted us to love and pray for our enemies as well (Matt. 5:43-46).

If all practised the natural love in all the various aspects of their lives, a brotherhood of man could be achieved, though it might not last. This is because the natural love is vulnerable to being weakened and even collapsing through human ambition for power, as well as material desires. Despite aspirations and hopes, people by themselves cannot bring about a permanent brotherhood as the human nature is subject to retrogression into hatred, war, and oppression of others. Therefore the natural love is inadequate to bring humans into a condition of full happiness on earth.

A time will come, however, when humanity will be universally restored to its original state of purity and freedom from sin. Then the brotherhood of man will exist in a degree of perfection that will make all humans happy.

Humans of and by themselves do not possess a divine element within them, though their souls are made in God's image and their life is sustained by the spirit of life emanating from God to all Creation. This absence of the divine within humans can, however, be changed as the next chapter shows.

Human Potential for Divinity

Man consists of body, soul and spirit – each made of different substance and functioning for a different length of time.

The *body* is material and temporary. After the end of the physical life, it will dissolve into its constituent elements and never again be resurrected in physical form. It shields the soul and spirit during the earthly life, but is not the real person, which is the soul. After death, the body ceases to be a part of the person altogether.

The *spirit* contains the functions of life and what controls the person's behavior. This includes the intellect, mental faculties, and reasoning powers. The spirit uses the organs of the material body to manifest these attributes. The spirit faculties, however, can function even when the brain or the physical organs of one or more of the five senses are impaired. The spirit doesn't die and continues in the spirit world after dropping the envelope of flesh. The mind – the mental and intellectual faculties – also continues, now without the limitations that the physical body had placed on it. Memory and all the things forming a person's identity continue too. The individual in the spirit world can still conceive thoughts of material things and perceive the physical – even more perfectly than before.

So after death, humans don't cease to live – they merely enter life on a different plane and in a different form. They retain everything of the mind, conscience and soul that was theirs in their earthly life. The spirit body continues to house and protect the soul.

The *soul* is the only part of man that is made in the image of its Creator. It therefore has the ability to partake of God's nature and substance and thus become immortal. This can happen as a result of transformation by the Divine Love – a higher form of love than the natural love with which humans are born. The Divine Love is only available from God through the longing of the soul.

When a soul receives the Divine Love and nature through faith and prayer, it begins to

Human Potential for Divinity

change from the image of God to the substance of God — which is how the transformation from humanity to divinity occurs. The person becomes a new creature and will have experienced a new birth (1 John 1:13; 3:6-8; 1 Pet. 1:23). With time, the person's nature becomes at one with the Father's nature. Then the individual is qualified to enter the Kingdom of God that Jesus taught about, or Celestial Heavens.

The soul is the essence of the human being. When it becomes transformed from humanity to divinity and enters God's Kingdom, the individual becomes a divine angel.

So to recap, without the Divine Love, humans are neither divine nor have God living in them. They are only created in the image of God and endowed with certain attributes of God, but not possessing the substance of God. This too applies only at the soul level, not the body level, for God does not possess a body in human shape. The new birth means that the soul, made in the image of God, is by the Divine Love transformed into the substance of God. The Bible also refers to this process as becoming a new creature / creation; being born again or born of God; and rebirth and renewal by the Holy Spirit (John 1:13; 2 Cor. 5:17; Gal. 6:15; 1 Pet. 1:23; Titus 3:5; 1 John 3:9 and 4:7).

Through the new birth, humans become at one with the Father. This happens because the Divine Love flowing into one's soul gradually replaces all that tends to sin and error. As the Divine Love takes over the soul, it changes it to the quality of the Great Soul of the Father. Thus the human becomes divine and immortal with their soul not only in the image of God, but also of divine substance. This, upon passing into the spirit world, enables them to enter the Celestial Kingdom of God.

Human Love versus Divine Love

God is Love and no human can come into a close personal relationship with Him (which is different from just being God's child by creation) unless they have His Love, the Divine Love, in their soul. This is what redeems humans from the way of sin and error that they are naturally prone to in their earthly life, and from sin's consequences in the spirit world.

The Divine Love can be freely obtained through sincere prayer in response to the longings of the soul (not just the desires of the mind and intellect), and faith that the Father will bestow it. The intellect cannot unite a person with God – only the soul, made in divine image or likeness, can make this connection. However, the likeness is only perfected by filling the soul with the Divine Love of the Father.

Love makes the whole universe run in harmony – without it, all would be chaos and unhappiness. Only the Divine Love can unite God and man, and enable humans to become divine angels with access to and abode in the Celestial Spheres.

The Holy Spirit is the sole instrument that can bring about the salvation of man by imparting the Divine Love into the soul. Without the Holy Spirit, no person can enter the Celestial Heaven. Resisting and rejecting the influence of the Holy Spirit consists of sin against the Spirit. As long as this persists, the person cannot be forgiven – it becomes the unforgivable sin (Matt. 12:32).

The Divine Love is an unconditional love regardless of the status of another being. It is the Love with which God loves the world. Jesus taught his disciples to love one another with the love that he had for them – which was the same as the Love that the Father loved him with (John 13:34-35; 15:9-13; 17:23). He also taught them to love and pray for their enemies. Doing this, they would be becoming perfect like the Father, who showers favors on both the just and the unjust, is perfect (Matt. 5:44-48). Growing in the likeness of the Father and experiencing their souls being transformed from the image of God into divine substance, they would be becoming more and more at one with God.

Human love is a mere shadow or image of the Divine Love. It is the love we are born with and develop as we grow up. It is manifested through, for example, motherly love, sibling love, married love, and love for friends. In expressing love to God, it is in obeying God's commandments – but may not go much beyond that as shown by the example of the rich young man who asked Jesus what was needed to inherit eternal life (Luke 18:18-27).

The natural love is not sufficient to enter the Kingdom of God – which is humanly impossible and can only come through God's help in the form of the Divine Love imparted by the Holy Spirit and resulting in soul transformation and the new birth (Matt. 19:16-26).

The natural love needs to be absorbed by the Divine Love. If humans, both in their physical life and when they enter the spirit world after death, refuse to ask for and receive the Divine Love, they will remain separated from the Father (though still his dear children by creation and thus endowed with some of God's attributes). As a result, they will only experience the limited happiness – though great from their perspective – that the natural love affords them. In time, however, they will reach a limit to their growth and development, and in addition to their happiness, also experience a certain dissatisfaction.

If individuals are not awakened to the need for the Divine Love, there is nothing divine in them and they will remain in this state with no assurance of immortality or even ongoing life. Of course, their existence is sustained by the creating and life-giving Spirit – which is not God, but emanating from God – the universal energy or life force and consciousness in and behind all things (Acts 17:27-28).

It is possible for all to seek and receive the Divine Love, but each individual needs to ask for it. Because of the God-given free will, many will not choose the way of seeking it. Also, there may come a time when the privilege of obtaining the Divine Love will be withdrawn.

Human Love versus Divine Love

The harmony of the universe is not dependent upon all humans / spirits receiving the Divine Love (and many will not). This is because in the workings of God's laws of harmony on individual souls, all sin and error will eventually be eradicated and only truth will remain. However, the absence of sin doesn't mean that all will be equally happy. Those with only the natural love will not be as happy as those with the Divine Love. Yet despite these differences, there will be overall harmony throughout.

Adam and Eve, or the first humans, had the natural love and were relatively happy, but couldn't resist temptation. Those in the spirit world with only the natural love too may be subject to temptation and, if it is not resisted, to fall from their state of happiness. By contrast those with the Divine Love become a part of divinity – as if they were very God – and never be subject to temptation or unhappiness. They are destined to live as immortal sinless spirits or divine angels through all eternity in the presence of and at-one with the Father.

Prayer for Divine Love

Below is an example prayer for the Divine Love. It doesn't have to be prayed verbatim, but it can give ideas how to approach the Father who, even more than a loving earthly father, delights in giving good gifts to His children (Luke 11:11-13).

In effect, the prayer contains the basic truths given to humankind by Celestial Spirits. It is important to be consistent and continue to pray for the Divine Love as soul transformation doesn't happen all at once, but is a process. However, a formal prayer is not necessary – in fact just longings from the soul, not even expressed in words, are sufficient as the Father is more than happy to send the Holy Spirit to impart the Divine Love to those who desire it (Luke 11:13).

Our Father, who are in heaven, we recognize that You are all holy and loving and merciful, and that we are Your children, and not the subservient, sinful and depraved creatures that our false teachers would have us believe. That we are the greatest of Your creation, and the most wonderful of all Your handiworks, and the objects of Your great soul's Love and tenderest care.

That Your will is that we become at one with You, and partake of Your great Love which You have bestowed upon us through Your mercy and desire that we become, in truth, Your children, through Love, and not through the sacrifice and death of any of Your creatures.

We pray that You will open up our souls to the inflowing of Your Love, and that then may come Your Holy Spirit to bring into our souls Your Love in great abundance, until our souls shall be transformed into the very essence of Yourself; and that there may come to us faith — such faith as will cause us to realize that we are truly Your children and one with You in very substance and not in image only.

Let us have such faith as will cause us to know that You are our Father, and the bestower of every good and perfect gift, and that only we, ourselves, can prevent Your Love changing us from the mortal to the immortal.

Prayer for Divine Love

Let us never cease to realize that Your Love is waiting for each and all of us, and that when we come to You, in faith and earnest aspiration, Your Love will never be withheld from us.

Keep us in the shadow of Your Love every hour and moment of our lives, and help us to overcome all temptations of the flesh, and the influence of the powers of the evil ones, which so constantly surround us and endeavour to turn our thoughts away from You to the pleasures and allurements of this world.

We thank You for Your Love and the privilege of receiving it, and we believe that You are our Father — the loving Father who smiles upon us in our weakness, and is always ready to help us and take us to Your arms of Love.

We pray this with all the earnestness and longings of our souls, and trusting in Your Love, give You all the glory and honour and love that our finite souls can give. Amen.

Further Reading

http://universal-spirituality.net/

Angelic Revelations of Divine Truth, Vol. I

Angelic Revelations of Divine Truth, Vol. II

http://new-birth.net/padgetts-messages/the-gift-of-the-divine-love/

http://new-birth.net/topical-subjects/the-soul-transformation-process-achieving-the-new-birth-on-earth/

http://new-birth.net/life-after-death/the-spirit-heavens-and-kingdom-of-god/

Acknowledgements

First, I would like to thank God the Father, the Source of all things, as well as those in the Celestial Realms for enabling, inspiring and blessing this small publication.

I must also thank my husband, Alex, for his ever-present love and support. He is always ready to help and to give helpful advice.

I also want to thank my friends in the Divine Love community for their support and encouragement, in particular Rev. Dr. Michael Nedbal.

About the Author

Eva Peck has an international and Christian background and is an ordained minister in the Foundation Church of Divine Truth. Having lived and worked in Australia, the United States, Europe, Asia, and the Middle East, including teaching English as a foreign language, she has experienced a range of cultures, customs, and environments. She now draws on those experiences in her writing.

Eva has a Bachelor's Degree in Biological Sciences, a Graduate Diploma in Education, and a Master's Degree in Theology. Since her retirement from teaching, she has been devoting her time to spiritual pursuits. She has written and published a number of books on spiritual themes, as well as building and maintaining several websites.

Eva lives in Brisbane, Australia, with her husband, Alex.

For more information
on the theme of this book, visit
http://universal-spirituality.net/

About Pathway Publishing

Pathway Publishing, managed by Eva Peck, is dedicated to sharing truth and beauty by publishing books and producing websites that present what is true to life and reality, as well as what is lovely and inspirational. The goal is to not only provide sound information, but also to uplift the human spirit.

Pathway Publishing has a vision of enriching the life of readers here and now, as well as helping them on their path of enlightenment and spiritual transformation. The wisdom and experience of spiritual teachers, thinkers, and visionary writers from various backgrounds and faith traditions are recognized and valued.

Books produced by Pathway Publishing broadly fall into two categories – spirituality and the arts – and include:

- *Divine Reflections in Times and Seasons*, Eva Peck
- *Divine Reflections in Natural Phenomena*, Eva Peck

- *Divine Reflections in Living Things*, Eva Peck
- *Divine Insights from Human Life,* Eva Peck
- *Pathway to Life - Through the Holy Scriptures,* Eva and Alexander Peck
- *Journey to the Divine Within – Through Silence, Stillness and Simplicity,* Alexander and Eva Peck
- *Jesus' Gospel of God's Love*, Eva Peck
- *Abundant Living on Small Income*, Eva Peck
- *The Greatest Love*, Eva Peck
- *Salvation*, Eva Peck
- *Problem of Evil*, Eva Peck
- *Answers to Prayer*, Eva Peck
- *The Bible as a Guide to Life*, Eva Peck
- *Life After Death*, Eva Peck
- *Jesus Christ – A New Look at His Identity and Mission*, Eva Peck and Michael Nedbal
- *Fulfillments of Old Testament Types*, Eva Peck

- *Artistic Inspirations - Paintings of Jindrich Degen* arranged by Eva and Alexander Peck
- *Colour and Contrast – Artwork of Jindrich Degen* arranged by Eva and Alexander Peck
- *Faces and Forms Across Time – Artwork of Jindrich Degen*, arranged by Eva and Alexander Peck
- *Variations – Art Exhibition of Jindrich Degen*, arranged by Eva and Alex Peck
- *Floral and Nature Art – Photography of Jindrich Degen,* arranged by Eva and Alexander Peck
- *Nature's Beauty – Art Photography of Jindrich Degen*, arranged by Eva and Alex Peck

- *Volné verše,* Jindrich Degen (Czech poetry)
- *Verše pro dnešní dobu,* Jindrich Degen (Czech poetry)
- *Pardál za úplňku a jiné povídky*, Eva Vaníčková (Czech stories set mostly in Indonesia)

Pathway Publishing
Seeking truth and beauty

www.ingramcontent.com/pod-product-compliance
Lightning Source LLC
Chambersburg PA
CBHW070553300426
44113CB00011B/1898